NEWBERN LIBRARY

CHANGING SPACES

How an Abandoned Bank Became a Beloved Community Library

JULIE KNUTSON

CHERRY LAKE PRESS

Published in the United States of America by Cherry Lake Publishing Group
Ann Arbor, Michigan
www.cherrylakepublishing.com

Reading Adviser: Marla Conn, MS, Ed., Literacy specialist, Read-Ability, Inc.
Photo Credits: © Tim Hursley, cover, 1, 5, 6, 20, 23, 24, 28; © Everett Historical/Shutterstock.com, 9, 10, 12, 13; © Rex Wholster/Shutterstock.com, 14; © Ersler Dmitry/Shutterstock.com, 17; © Billvolckening/Wikimedia Commons, 18

Cherry Lake Press is an imprint of Cherry Lake Publishing Group.

Library of Congress Cataloging-in-Publication Data
Names: Knutson, Julie, author.
Title: Newbern Library / by Julie Knutson.
Description: Ann Arbor, Michigan : Cherry Lake Publishing, [2021]. | Series: Changing spaces | Includes index. | Audience: Grades 4-6 | Summary: "Learn more about how Alabama's Newbern Library went from empty bank building to vibrant library and community space. Explore the logistics of repurposing the building and meet the people who made it happen. The book showcases a range of 21st century skills—from "Flexibility & Adaptation" to "Creativity & Innovation"—and shows how moving away from a tear-down culture towards one of reuse helps tackle a host of critical challenges facing our planet and population. Thought-provoking questions and hands-on activities encourage the development of critical life skills and social emotional growth. Books in this series include table of contents, glossary of key words, index, author biography, sidebars, and infographics"—Provided by publisher.
Identifiers: LCCN 2020006368 (print) | LCCN 2020006369 (ebook) | ISBN 9781534169029 (hardcover) | ISBN 9781534170704 (paperback) | ISBN 9781534172548 (pdf) | ISBN 9781534174382 (ebook)
Subjects: LCSH: Newbern Public Library (Newbern, Ala.)—Juvenile literature. | Library buildings—Alabama—Newbern—Juvenile literature. | Bank buildings—Remodeling for other use—Alabama—Newbern—Juvenile literature. | Newbern (Ala.)—Buildings, structures, etc.—Juvenile literature.
Classification: LCC Z733.N796 K59 2020 (print) | LCC Z733.N796 (ebook) | DDC 022/.30976143—dc23
LC record available at https://lccn.loc.gov/2020006368
LC ebook record available at https://lccn.loc.gov/2020006369

Cherry Lake Publishing Group would like to acknowledge the work of the Partnership for 21st Century Learning, a Network of Battelle for Kids. Please visit http://www.battelleforkids.org/networks/p21 for more information.

Printed in the United States of America
Corporate Graphics

With thanks to Andrew Freear and Natalie Butts-Ball of Rural Studio

ABOUT THE AUTHOR

Julie Knutson is an author/educator fascinated by the endless ways in which people and communities can transform old spaces for new uses. She lives in Illinois with her husband, son, and extremely energetic border collie.

TABLE OF CONTENTS

Adaptive Reuse–More Than Meets the Eye

Essential question: *How do communities—and the people and buildings within them—adjust to changing times?*

It's a sleepy Saturday morning in Newbern, Alabama, a tiny town of just 172 people located in Hale County. Customers duck into Newbern Mercantile, the only store on the main street, to gather weekend breakfast supplies. No sirens blare at the firehouse; all is quiet at Town Hall. But the Newbern Library is abuzz with activity as young makers and STEM explorers gather and grow in numbers.

The Newbern Library is an important community space in its tiny Alabama town.

Happiness Is a Warm . . . Library?

Researchers find that cities and towns with well-resourced libraries have happier citizens. Surveys show that 65 percent of Americans feel that libraries help them grow as people. Two-thirds of Americans feel that the closure of their public library would have a major negative impact on their community.

What unused spaces in your town could be adaptively reused?

Just a few years before, this old bank building stood empty. The unheated structure found occasional use on Election Day and for city council meetings. But visionary residents saw its potential to serve as a place that could change lives as a library. It could do so, in the words of town postmaster Frances Sullivan, by reopening its doors "to tutoring, mentoring, after-school programs, and summer programs." It could be a place where kids could learn about everything from aerospace to zoology. It could be a place where residents of all ages could create and share ideas. It would provide a vital anchor in the community where people could "bank on" the power of reading and invest in the "currency" of knowledge.

How did this building, which was shuttered during the **Great Depression**, come to have a new life? Who had the idea to reinvent this long-unoccupied but much-beloved brick structure as a library? Why was this seen as necessary for the well-being of residents? And who partnered to **adaptively reuse** this space?

Read on to discover how longtime Newbern residents and a group of architecture students worked together to reimagine a new use for the unused space. In the process, learn how communities of all sizes can adapt treasured spaces for changing times, preserving histories and paving the way toward more **resilient** futures.

Hale County During the Great Depression

The Great Depression (1929–1939) was a decade-long economic downturn. During this period, **sharecroppers** *in Hale County were struck particularly hard by poverty and unemployment. Around the time that Newbern's bank closed in 1936, the writer-photographer team of James Agee and Walker Evans traveled throughout Hale County to document living conditions. Their work became one of the most well-known photographic collections of the 20th century, "Let Us Now Praise Famous Men."*

CHAPTER 1

Rooted in Place

Like many towns across the Black Belt—a region so-nicknamed because of its rich, fertile soil—Newbern's economy was built around cotton farming. Plantations dotted the surrounding countryside. These agricultural estates were owned by white people who became wealthy on the backs of the enslaved people who worked in the fields.

A high-demand cash crop, cotton made up half of U.S. **exports** in the first part of the 19th century. Alabama was a major grower. During this period, the port of Mobile was the nation's third busiest

Much of Alabama's cotton industry relied on the labor of enslaved people until the practice was abolished in 1865.

Racial discrimination and segregation were widespread in the south through much of the 20th century. Effects of this era are still felt today.

after New York and New Orleans. Even after the Civil War and during **Reconstruction**, cotton fields continued to be farmed under the sharecropping system.

The Bank of Newbern opened in 1906, at a time when racial segregation was legal under **Jim Crow laws**. At that time—and until the bank closed in the 1930s—legislation prevented black residents from having bank accounts or receiving loans. Other spaces in the community, from the mercantile store to its hotel, were governed by the same set of segregationist policies.

The Great Migration

Between about 1916 and 1970, more than 6 million African Americans migrated from the rural South to industrial northern cities. Between 1910 and 1920, the number of black residents in Philadelphia grew by 500 percent and in Detroit by 611 percent. The "push" factors behind this exodus from the South were widespread violence, racial segregation, and lack of economic opportunity. The "pull" factors toward the North were the promises of high wages and better living standards.

Many farmers from across the South and Midwest were ruined in the Great Depression, contributing to the economic crisis.

Bread lines in New York City were set up to help feed families during the Depression.

Hale County's economy collapsed under the weight of the Great Depression. The Bank of Newbern went with it. As the community tried to rebuild its economic foundations in the 1940s, the building found use as a livestock feed store. Later, it was briefly used as an insurance office.

Alabama is home to a number of sites important in the civil rights movement.

But Newbern was shrinking as residents of all races left it behind—pushed out by limited opportunities and pulled by the promise of a better life elsewhere. Banks and businesses didn't have the client base to support them. Newbern shrank from a peak population of 564 in 1900 to 316 by 1960. The population continued to decline, dropping to 186 by 2010.

A Safe House on the Civil Rights Trail

Hale County was central to the civil rights movement of the 1950s and 1960s. The movement developed not just in the urban centers of Montgomery, Selma, and Birmingham, but also in rural communities at their outskirts. That history is documented at the Safe House Black History Museum in Greensboro. In 2010, Rural Studio students worked with museum founder Theresa Burroughs to renovate the historic house museum. Here in this building, just 2 weeks before he was assassinated in 1968, Martin Luther King Jr. found refuge from the Ku Klux Klan.

CHAPTER 2

The Power of Architecture to Address Community Challenges

In the early 1990s, a group of 12 Auburn University architecture students and their professor, Samuel Mockbee, set out on a yearlong experiment. The goal was to use their profession to address social challenges in rural Hale County, where one in four people live below the poverty line. These problems included lack of access to quality, affordable housing. Mockbee believed that architecture needed to be *less* about the architect and *more* about the people and communities that architects served. Architecture and design, he thought, should improve the lives of all people, not just the world's wealthiest few.

Most high-end architecture can only be enjoyed by the very wealthy.

The quilts of Gee's Bend have been celebrated as artistic masterpieces all over the world.

In 1994, the team completed its first design-build project, a home for the Bryant family in Mason's Bend, Alabama. With that project, the foundations for Rural Studio—which relied on "close and respectful client relationships" and community partnerships—were firmly laid. Innovative building methods, reuse of materials, and an emphasis on making structures that met client needs marked the program's work.

The Quilters of Gee's Bend

About an hour southeast of Newbern lies Boykin, Alabama, home to the critically acclaimed Gee's Bend Quilters Collective. For more than a century, the African-American quilters of Gee's Bend have practiced their own form of adaptive reuse. They turn salvaged fiber scraps into modernist masterpieces that provide not only warmth and comfort, but also an outlet for creative expression.

Their colorful, abstract blankets made of pieces of rescued textiles—recycled clothing, feed sacks, found fabrics—gained worldwide attention in the mid-20th century. The quilts made here are both the works of individuals and the product of collaboration.

In recent years, works made by the Gee's Bend Quilters have been displayed in locations ranging from New York to San Francisco. They've adorned envelopes as postage stamps and inspired new quilters to take needle to fabric. Still, the broader Boykin community faces major challenges that plague other rural areas: poverty, lack of jobs, and limited educational opportunities.

The Rural Studio "emphasizes place, beauty, economy, purpose, and dignity in all that we do, from education to research to outreach."

Community members, including Newbern postmaster Frances Sullivan, took notice. A Hale County native, Frances left the area in the 1970s. She returned in 1993, around the same time that Rural Studio arrived in town.

The changes that Rural Studio brought to Newbern didn't go unnoticed by Frances. In 1993, she remembers, "downtown Newbern consisted of four vacant businesses, one general store, and the post office." She watched as new life was breathed into three of the four vacant buildings.

As for the fourth? Frances had an idea, a vision. It involved adapting, reusing, and giving new life to Newbern's old, unused, and elegant bank building.

CHAPTER 3

A Library for Today and Tomorrow

Since 2001, Andrew Freear has directed Rural Studio's programs. For the majority of those years, Frances Sullivan badgered him to transform the old bank building into a library. Until the Town Hall was completed in 2011, the unheated, empty bank was occasionally brought back to service for voting and council meetings. But with a new space in which to fulfill those civic functions, new uses for the old building could be envisioned. Frances's effort to secure a community library seemed even more urgent after the local school library closed as part of district **consolidation**. A place to access and exchange information was sorely needed.

The new library space would still honor the building's history.

The Rural Studio wanted to be sure the library was as functional as possible.

In Frances's mind, the former bank would make a perfect library. She and four other community members—including former school librarians and teachers—petitioned Freear to get the project on the Rural Studio **docket**. The studio took on the adaptive reuse challenge, promising to honor the structure while modernizing it to serve a new purpose.

A rental fee of $1 per year

Rural Studio and the town of Newbern worked with the family that owns the old bank to negotiate a lease agreement. The family transferred the space over to the town's care for $1 per year, on the condition that it remains a library.

Students didn't set to work right away. Instead, the fifth-year students spent a month investigating three different community project sites. Then, they divided themselves into teams of four. Over the next 975 days, this team—consisting of Morgan Acino, Ashley Clark, Stephen Durham, and Will Gregory—oversaw the planning, design, and construction of the new library. They helped fundraise. They met with librarians and representatives from other communities to fully understand the function of a public library.

A Varied Portfolio of Community-Based Projects

Today, Rural Studio welcomes approximately 40 students a year. Over the past 3 decades, its students have worked across Hale County on a range of community projects. In addition to the library, student teams have designed and built Newbern's firehouse and town hall. They've also ushered animal shelters, learning centers, boys and girls clubs, and public parks from concept to reality. As with the Newbern Library, these idea proposals often come from civic leaders and residents.

Since 2005, visiting students have embraced the challenge of designing a house that could be built for $20,000. The studio also engages with sustainability and food justice issues through its student-run farm and design-build support for local farmers' markets.

They listened to residents' wish lists for the exterior, mindful that the desire was more for a "repurposing" that maintained the historic look of the building. They referenced archival photos and isolated features—like its simple canopy—for the building's 21st-century reboot.

Then, they set on the task of designing and building the interior. It was important to the community that features of the old bank be maintained. Today, the building's original purpose is evident in the safe door that greets visitors upon entrance. The librarian's desk also harkens back to the previous use as the teller's counter. The courtyard and garden area were created from the 8,200 red bricks that had lined the vault and were carefully removed by hand. An extension in the back of the building houses a larger collection of books.

Access to an engaging library space improves community life in Newbern.

The interior of the library features both public and private spaces. In the large middle section, communal events like group knitting sessions, public talks, and STEM Saturdays occur. Computers are available, allowing for high-speed internet access in a region where it is sometimes spotty. The library also offers private, partitioned reading areas for study and work. The town's youngest readers even have the option of crawling up into a carpet-lined children's space, where they can embark on reading adventures with their favorite characters.

For Newberners, the joy of this building comes in accepting what it was and delighting in its transformation. It's a space where the governing currency—now and for the foreseeable future—is knowledge, creativity, and community conversation. It's a place where you can safely "bank on reading."

Extend Your Learning

Brick-and-mortar libraries aren't the only ways that people can access books. Around the world, innovative librarians and book lovers have used animals and vehicles to deliver books to readers in off-the-beaten-path locations. Two of these figures were Mary Lemist Titcomb and Luis Soriano.

Look up biographies of both of them. When and where did each of them live? How did they deliver books to patrons? Why did they think it was important to provide access to books? How did their efforts change lives? Are there outreach efforts similar to theirs in your community?

Glossary

adaptively reuse (uh-DAP-tiv-lee ree-YOOZ) to reuse a structure for a purpose other than that which it was originally designed to serve

consolidation (kuhn-sah-lih-DAY-shuhn) the act of bringing several different parts together into one

docket (DAHK-it) a calendar of business matters to be acted on

exports (EK-sports) materials or goods sent to another country for sale

Great Depression (GRAYT dih-PRESH-uhn) a period of global economic decline that lasted from 1929 until 1939

Jim Crow laws (JIM KROH LAWZ) laws in the United States that legalized segregation from the late-19th to mid-20th centuries and set different rules for black and white Americans

Reconstruction (ree-kuhn-STRUHK-shuhn) the period immediately following the Civil War when states that had left the Union returned and were reorganized

resilient (ree-ZIL-yuhnt) able to recover from difficulty

sharecroppers (SHAIR-krahp-erz) tenant farmers who worked the land and received a share of the value of the crops minus what was owed

INDEX